50 Fun-Filled
DRAW & WRITE
PROMPTS

by Alyse Sweeney

SCHOLASTIC
PROFESSIONAL BOOKS

NEW YORK • TORONTO • LONDON • AUCKLAND • SYDNEY
MEXICO CITY • NEW DELHI • HONG KONG

Cover design by Norma Ortiz
Interior illustrations by James Graham Hale
Interior design by Solutions by Design, Inc.

ISBN: 0-439-10615-X

Contents

Introduction

Welcome to *50 Fun-Filled Draw & Write Prompts*! These appealing reproducible pages pair drawing prompts with quick companion writing prompts on topics kids know and love: favorite animals, friends, family members, special events, playtime, school, and more. Each page invites children to create a drawing about a topic before putting their ideas into words. Kids love to draw because it gives them the freedom to express themselves creatively. As a pre-writing warm-up, drawing sparks kids' interest, helps them generate ideas and details for writing, and makes their subjects lively and real.

The variety of fun formats in this book encourages children to produce varied types of writing: personal, interactive, informative, and creative. Beginning writers flourish when given the opportunity to write about topics that are important to them and that they know about. Through personal writing, kids draw upon their own experiences, surroundings, and preferences. Interactive writing, such as Draw & Write Greeting Cards, fosters relationships with others. Children are able to show what they know about various topics through informative writing. In Color & Write and Connect the Dots & Write, children first discover a hidden picture and then use prior knowledge to write about topics such as animals, ice cream, and sports. Students also produce creative writing when they write stories about various animals and their own imaginary creature.

50 Fun-Filled Draw & Write Prompts provides students with fun and motivating opportunities to write, and also helps children recognize that they have something worthwhile to say. Giving children opportunities to share their writing helps them gain confidence as writers. It also allows them to build fluency and develop their reading skills. Encourage children to share their Draw & Write Prompts both at school and at home. Family members will particularly enjoy "My Family Members" on page 24 and any of the Draw & Write Greeting Cards on pages 38–43.

50 Fun-Filled Draw & Write Prompts engages beginning writers of all ability levels. So jump right in and watch your students develop enthusiasm and confidence as writers!

How to Use This Book

The reproducible Draw & Write pages are grouped together by format (bookmarks, charts, interviews, and so on). You can use the pages in any order. You'll find that Draw & Write Prompts are easy to integrate into your curriculum. For example, Draw & Write All About Me pages are perfect for getting to know each other at the beginning of the school year; "Amazing Animals" on page 25 ties in nicely with a unit on animal studies; and Draw & Write Cartoons enhance character education. You'll find specific suggestions for using each prompt on pages 6–11.

Pre-Writing

Choose a Draw & Write page and make enough copies for your class. Set the stage for writing by discussing the topic. A pre-writing discussion helps students activate prior knowledge. Then give each child a copy of the reproducible page, crayons, and pencils. Read the directions aloud and show students where to draw on the page. As children are drawing, encourage them to add details that may later help them in their writing.

After students have finished with their drawings, you may wish to give them an opportunity to talk about what they have drawn. They can describe their drawing to you, a partner, a small group, or the whole class. This will also help them generate ideas for their writing.

Writing

Read the prompts aloud so that children are clear about what they will be writing. The prompts are easily adapted to different levels of writing development. You may wish to brainstorm as a class a list of possible responses and write them on chart paper or on the chalkboard. When students are writing, they can refer to the list for ideas or for help with spelling. Children can also refer to the word banks on many pages to guide them as they are writing.

Sharing

Children will experience many benefits when they share their writing with their classmates, teachers, families, and others. When children share their writing, they see themselves as writers, develop reading skills, and build fluency. And because the prompts capture the thoughts, experiences, and interests of the writer, they provide a tremendous opportunity for students to get to know each other. Children will see that there are things they have in common with others and that each person is a unique individual.

Collaborative Class Books

When students have completed their prompt page, bind the pages together to make a collaborative class book. For example, you can make a book of Amazing Animal Charts or Imaginary Creature Creations. Invite a student to decorate a cover, and then add the book to your classroom library. Have students take turns bringing home the book in a resealable plastic bag to share with family members.

Getting Started With
Draw & Write Prompts

DRAW & WRITE BOOKMARKS

Draw & Write Bookmarks are a great way to motivate kids to read. The three bookmarks invite children to draw and then generate a list related to their picture. Lists are an important writing format that can help children organize ideas for writing. When children have completed their bookmarks, they can use their lists to generate longer, more detailed pieces.

"I Can..." Bookmark

Brainstorm with children a list of things that they can do. Students may know how to play a certain game, write stories, help a parent cook dinner, or draw a shark. Ask students to think about how they learned these skills. Did someone teach them? Did they practice and learn on their own? Lead a discussion about things students would like to learn how to do. Make a list on chart paper for students to refer to during the year. They can write their initials beside skills on the list as they learn them.

"I Like to..." Bookmark

As a class, generate a list of activities that children like to do. Encourage children to think about things they like to do at school, at home, in after-school programs, at camp, or elsewhere. They may like to play soccer, write poems, read to a sibling, or play with a pet. Elicit from children reasons why they like to do these activities. For example, do they like to play soccer because they like to run, be outside, spend time with their teammates, or all three?

"I Like to Read About..." Bookmark

Brainstorm with children lists of topics they like to read about. Direct their attention to the illustration on the page and to books around the classroom for ideas. They may like to read about planets, animals, friends, families, funny things, sports, and so on. Ask children to think about books that they read at home as well.

If you have students who tend to read the same books or same types of books, this bookmark may help them expand their reading preferences. Hearing what their classmates like to read about may also motivate them to try new books or topics.

DRAW & WRITE ALL ABOUT ME

Each page in this section focuses on an aspect of children's immediate world, enabling them to write about who they are. The writing format is straightforward and the pages provide generous space for drawing. These prompts are a great way for children to learn about each other at the beginning of the year. When students have completed all nine pages in this section, they can assemble the pages and make a cover for an All About Me book.

My Hands/My Feet

Ask children to think about the many things that they can do with their hands and feet. Have them think about how they use their hands and feet both in and out of school (writing, painting, running, jumping, and so on). Children can use the word bank on each page to help them as they are writing.

For an extension, have children trace their

hands and feet on colored paper and cut out the outlines. Ask them to write an action word in the outline that is something they can do with either their hands or their feet. Display them on a bulletin board entitled "We Can!"

My Teeth

Children will need small mirrors to draw a picture of their smile. After they draw their smile, they will record how many teeth they have lost so far. Emphasize that children should not worry or be upset if they have not lost any teeth yet. They will soon! Brainstorm as a group why teeth are important. Ask students to think about how difficult it would be to eat without teeth. Ask them what sorts of food babies eat and why. Demonstrate that teeth also help us say some sounds, like the *th* sound in *tooth* and *teeth*!

Munch, Munch, Munch!

After children draw their favorite foods on the large plate on this page, they write about their food preferences. Have children share one food they like and one food they dislike as a pre-writing warm-up. This page ties in well with a study of nutrition. Lead a discussion about what kinds of foods are nutritious, and ask children if the food they drew is nutritious.

My Favorite Toy

Encourage students to use details in both their drawing and their written description of their favorite toy. Model for the class a detailed description of a toy by telling about your favorite toy when you were a child. When students have completed their Draw & Write page, they can play "20 Questions" to guess each other's toys. They can ask questions such as, "Is your toy soft?" or "Does it have wheels?"

My Room

On this page, children draw a picture of their room and write about what they do there. Have children brainstorm the activities that they do in their rooms, such as sleep, play with toys, read, write, and get dressed. Encourage

children to use the details in their drawing to help them as they are writing. As an extension, discuss the activities that typically take place in other rooms of a home.

Playing Outside/Playing Inside

What are your students' favorite outdoor and indoor activities? On these pages, they'll draw and then write about playing outside and inside. Have a discussion about how the weather and seasons affect what types of games your students play. What do they play when it is warm? Cold? Rainy? Snowy?

My Friend, _____

Have children write their friend's name on the line in the title. Then invite them to draw a picture of their friend. As a class, generate a list of words that describe friends (*caring, funny, generous, cheerful, helpful*, and so on.) Encourage students to think about what activities they like to do with their friend at school or at home. This page can lead into a discussion about what makes a good friend and how children can be good friends to others.

DRAW & WRITE CHARTS

Draw & Write Charts give students an opportunity to write about their family, favorite animals, and favorite books in a chart format. Charts require students to cluster, or categorize, information. This is a helpful organizational skill for students to use in their writing. Model for children how to fill in a chart before they begin.

After children have completed these three charts, have them create their own charts. Help them choose a broad topic such as favorite foods, activities, games, places, and so on.

My Family Members

Ask students to choose family members to draw and then write about. Encourage children to consider extended relatives, such as grandparents, aunts, uncles, and cousins. Show students the line in each box on which to write the family member's name. This is a nice send-home activity that family members will enjoy reading.

Amazing Animals

This chart works well as a pre-writing activity for an animal report. Children choose two of their favorite animals to draw; then they write one interesting fact and one thing they would like to learn about each animal. When children complete their chart, have them research the fact that they wanted to know.

My Favorite Books

For this chart, children choose two of their favorite books to draw. In the space provided, they can draw the book cover or a character or scene from the book. Children then write a sentence stating what each book is about and a sentence describing their favorite part of each book. This chart is a good introduction to writing a simple book report because it requires specific and succinct information. Have children use their charts to write or dictate a book report on one of their books. Display the charts in your classroom or school library to help students make book selections.

DRAW & WRITE SEQUENCING

In this section, students write the steps to do three everyday activities. As they draw and write about each step, children develop important sequencing skills.

When students have finished these pages, make a sequencing game about one of the activities (brushing teeth, getting ready for bed, and so on). Write each step on an index card. Working with partners, students read the cards and arrange the steps in order. For younger students, draw a picture on each card to guide their reading.

Brushing My Teeth

Begin by discussing the steps involved in brushing teeth. It is helpful to bring in a toothbrush and toothpaste and demonstrate the steps for children. Have students choose four steps and draw each one in a box. The steps can be very simple, such as "Put toothpaste on my toothbrush, brush my teeth, rinse my mouth," and so on. This activity ties in nicely with a unit on health.

Getting Ready for Bed/ Getting Ready for School

Begin by having your students share the steps they take to get ready for bed and to get ready for school. Students can organize their writing in a graphic organizer as a pre-writing warm-up. You may wish to model this for students first.

DRAW & WRITE INTERVIEWS

There are two parts to each Draw & Write Interview. On the first page, children draw a picture about a specified topic and write about it. On the second page, children draw themselves beside an interviewer. Students read the interviewer's question in the speech balloon and write a response in their own speech balloon. Cartoons and speech balloons are highly motivating to children and help them visualize the interview. There are additional interview questions below each cartoon. You may wish to show students examples of comic strips so that they will better understand how speech balloons work. As an extension, have students conduct interviews with each other or with students in other classes. As a group, think of topics for the interviews and generate questions. Students can interview their partner in front of the class or in front of a small group.

My School/My School Interview

After students draw a picture of their school, ask them to look at their drawings to help them think of words that describe their school. What is their favorite place at school: the library, cafeteria, playground, or elsewhere? Finally, have them think of one special thing about their school. Remind them that it can be anything: a special person, event, place, or even the feeling that they get when they are at school. On the interview page, show students where to draw themselves in the cartoon. Help them read the interviewer's question and explain that they should write a response in the speech balloon. Then have them respond to the additional interview questions below the cartoon.

Happy Halloween!/ A Halloween Interview

Students begin by drawing something they like to do on Halloween and then writing about it. On the next page, they draw themselves in their Halloween costume next to the interviewer. If children do not yet know what they will be for Halloween, they can draw what they would like to be for Halloween or what they were last year. Ask students to think about why they chose their costume. Is the costume scary or funny? Is it different than last year or the same? Encourage them to use their pictures to decide what is their favorite part of their costume.

My Favorite Animal/ My Favorite Animal Interview

After students draw a picture of their favorite animal, have them answer the questions about the animal's size, color, habitat, and so on. This activity can lead into a mini-report about their animal. On the next page, children draw themselves being interviewed by a zookeeper about their favorite animal. Ask students to think about why they like this animal so much. Is it because it can do cool things, like change colors or catch insects with its tongue? If children have trouble answering the last question about an interesting fact, help them find a fact in a book or encourage them to write about a physical characteristic.

My Favorite Place/ My Favorite Place Interview

Students begin by drawing a picture of their favorite place and writing about it. If they have trouble thinking of a place, work together to list places in your community, such as a park, library, public pool, or skating rink. On the next page, students draw themselves beside the interviewer and respond to questions about their favorite place. As a follow-up, ask children where they would like to visit that they have not been to before?

DRAW & WRITE GREETING CARDS

With Draw & Write Greeting Cards, children write and decorate cards for special people in their lives. This helps children see that the written language can be used to reach out and connect to other people. Discuss with children about how nice it feels to receive cards and how they will be making other people happy by sending them. Children can hand deliver their cards, but it is also fun to mail them. Model for children how to address an envelope and where to put the stamp. You can also set up a mail station in your classroom with a mailbox for each student. Leave supplies in the station for children to send letters and cards to their classmates. As an extension, children may want to make and send cards to people in hospitals or nursing homes. Greeting cards from your students are a great way to bring cheer to others in the community.

For each of the six Draw & Write Greeting Cards, show students how to fold the paper to assemble the card (directions appear on the card). Have children draw a picture related to the card in the box on the front. On the inner left side of the card, have children respond to the short writing prompt. The writing prompts on the inner right side are more open-ended.

You may wish to brainstorm possible messages with children before they begin writing. If children have extra time, encourage them to draw a picture on the back of the card as well.

Send home Draw & Write Greeting Cards for Thanksgiving, winter holidays, and Valentine's Day. Keep extra copies on hand of the Thank You card, Happy Birthday card, and Congratulations card. Encourage children to make these cards for classmates and family members whenever the occasion arises.

DRAW & WRITE CARTOONS

D raw & Write Cartoons encourage children to think about how to resolve conflicts peacefully. The speech balloons and cartoons generate children's interest and prompt them to think about how they would respond in that situation. Draw & Write Cartoons are ideal for lessons on character education.

As an extension, children can share their completed Draw & Write Cartoons by role-playing with a partner. Role-playing these situations is also an excellent way for your students to develop and practice conflict-resolution skills.

Let's Share

Read the speech balloon aloud and ask children to think about how they would feel if someone asked for something in the way Tim did. Have students think about how they can respond nicely to Tim. Invite them to draw themselves in the box and write their response in the speech balloon. Ask children to think of how Tim might have asked for the crayon in a nicer way, such as, "May I use that crayon when you are done?" or "Please tell me when you are done with that crayon so that I can use it." They can write additional responses on the back of the page.

Making Up

Read the speech balloon aloud with your class. Ask students to think about how they would feel if someone broke their toy. What do they think the other person could say to make them feel better? What kind of responses would make them feel worse, such as "So!" or "I don't care." Next have students draw themselves in the cartoon and write in the speech balloon what they would say to Samantha to make her feel better. Responses may include, "I'm sorry," "Let me help you glue it together," or "I didn't mean to break your toy. It was an accident."

Playing Together

Have students draw themselves in the cartoon playing a game. Ask them how they think the child that is left out feels. What would they say if their friend asked if he or she could play also? Responses may include, "I'm going to ask my friend to play with us," or "Let's invite my friend to play too."

Be a Problem Solver!

On this page, children make up a situation in which two children are having a problem. Then, they write down their solution. Guide children through this exercise by reminding them of conflicts that were resolved peacefully in the classroom or on the playground. Or, brainstorm together areas of the classroom where potential conflicts may take place, such as a computer station where children have to take turns. This open-ended activity works well as a follow-up to the other Draw & Write Cartoons.

COLOR & WRITE

I n this section, children color by number to discover a hidden object in each picture. They then use prior knowledge to write about what they know about the object. The word bank guides children to write factual information, making this section a good introduction to report writing.

Read the instructions aloud with your

students. Emphasize that they are asked to write three facts about flowers. Model the difference between fact and opinion. For example, "I think flowers are pretty" states an opinion, whereas "Flowers come in many colors" states a fact. Similarly, "I had ice cream last night" is a personal statement, whereas "Ice cream is cold, but can melt fast" shows what the child knows about ice cream.

As an extension, have children produce personal writing on one of the topics. For example, students may write about their favorite flavor of ice cream, where they have eaten ice cream, or an ice cream cake they once had at a birthday. Have students share both pieces of writing with the class. Discuss the different type of information given in each piece.

CONNECT THE DOTS & WRITE

In this section, children will enjoy connecting the dots to reveal animal drawings: a spider, a starfish, and a pair of monkeys. After they discover the animals, children answer questions about them. Children can make their own connect-the-dot surprises by drawing a picture in light pencil and then adding dots and numbers in pen or marker. When the ink has dried, they can erase the pencil. Have children trade their connect-the-dot pictures with a partner and complete them. Then they can write or narrate a short story about the pictures.

DRAW & WRITE STEP BY STEP

Each of these Draw & Write prompts has two pages. The first page shows how to draw an animal in six easy steps. It is a good idea to give children scrap paper on which to practice drawing the steps. Remind children that the steps are only a guide; children can draw the

animal in their own style if they wish. When they are ready, they can draw the animal on the second page and color it. The writing prompts at the bottom of the second page form a fill-in-the-blank creative story. Kids fill in the missing information with their own imaginative ideas. They'll enjoy sharing their stories and hearing how each one is unique.

DRAW & WRITE CREATURES

Children use their imagination to create their own made-up creature. On the first page, they draw the creature in the box and then answer questions about it. The questions will help children organize their thoughts for the writing to come on the next page. Encourage children to think of more questions about their creatures and answer them on the back of the page. This section is a good introduction to pre-writing. On the second page, kids make up a mini-story by drawing four things that happen to their creature. Below each drawing, they write a description of the event. Remind children to refer to their writing on the first page as they are writing their mini-story. This activity can serve as a graphic organizer to write a longer, more detailed story. Depending upon their literacy development, children can either write, dictate, or narrate a story about their creature.

As an extension, have children make three-dimensional versions of their creatures with clay. Display the clay creatures along with children's creative stories.

"I Can..."
BOOKMARK

by _____

Think about all the things that you can do.

In the circle, draw one thing that you can do.

On the lines, write four things that you can do.

Cut out your bookmark along the dotted lines.

In the circle, draw what you can do.

I can _____

_____

I can _____

_____

I can _____

_____

I can _____

_____

"I Like to..."
BOOKMARK

by _____

Think about all the things that you like to do.

In the circle, draw one thing that you like to do.

On the lines, write four things that you like to do.

Cut out your bookmark along the dotted lines.

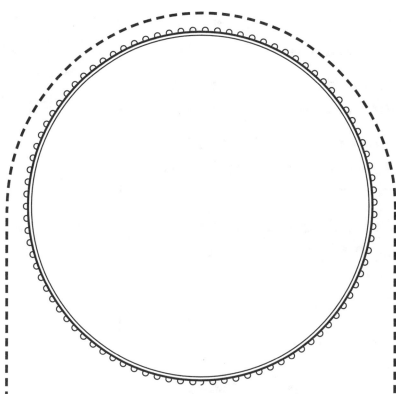

In the circle, draw something you like to do.

I like to _____

_____

I like to _____

_____

I like to _____

_____

I like to _____

_____

"I Like to Read About..."
BOOKMARK

by _____

Think about all the things that you like to read about.

In the book, draw one thing that you like to read about.

On the lines, write four things that you like to read about.

Cut out your bookmark along the dotted lines.

In the book, draw something you like to read about.

I like to read about...

1. _____

   _____

2. _____

   _____

3. _____

   _____

4. _____

   _____

My Hands

by _____

Trace your hand in the box below.

These are three things that I can do with my hands.

I can _____

_____

I can _____

_____

I can _____

_____

WORD BANK

touch

tickle

clap

snap

draw

point

wave

write

My Feet

by _____

Trace your foot in the box below.

These are three things that I can do with my feet.

I can _____

_____

I can _____

_____

I can _____

_____

50 Fun-Filled Draw & Write Prompts Scholastic Professional Books

My Teeth

by _____

Look in the mirror to see what your teeth look like. Then draw a picture of your smile in the box below.

So far, I have lost _____ teeth.

I am glad I have teeth because

_____

_____

_____

_____

WORD BANK

chew

bite

crunch

munch

eat

wiggle

brush

Munch, Munch, Munch!

by _____

Draw your favorite foods on the plate.

I like to eat _____.

But I don't like to eat _____.

_____ and _____ taste good together.

_____ and _____ do *not* taste good together!

50 Fun-Filled Draw & Write Prompts Scholastic Professional Books

My Favorite Toy

 by _____

Draw your favorite toy in the box below.

```
┌─────────────────────────────────────────────┐
│                                             │
│                                             │
│                                             │
│                                             │
│                                             │
│                                             │
│                                             │
│                                             │
│                                             │
└─────────────────────────────────────────────┘
```

My favorite toy is _____

These are words that describe my favorite toy:

_____

_____

It is my favorite toy because

_____

_____

WORD BANK

fun

soft

play

share

doll

truck

game

My Room

by _____

Draw a picture of your room in the box below.

[ ]

These are words that describe my room:

_____

_____

These are things in my room:

_____

_____

This is something I like to do in my room. I like to

_____

_____

WORD BANK

bed

chair

toys

books

window

table

lamp

clean

messy

50 Fun-Filled Draw & Write Prompts Scholastic Professional Books

Playing Outside

by _____

This is a picture of me playing outside.

What are you playing?

I am playing _____

I like to play this because _____

_____

Are you playing with a friend or by yourself?

I am playing _____

Playing Inside

by _____

This is a picture of me playing inside.

```



```

What are you playing?

I am playing _____

I like to play this because _____

_____

Are you playing with a friend or by yourself?

I am playing _____

I like to play inside when _____

_____

50 Fun-Filled Draw & Write Prompts Scholastic Professional Books

My Friend, _____

by _____

This is a picture of my friend.

These are words that describe my friend.

_____

_____

This is something my friend and I like to do together.

We like to _____

I like my friend because _____

_____

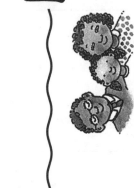

My Family Members

by _____

Draw a picture of two people in your family in the boxes. Write the name of each person below your drawing. Then fill in the chart.

Draw a picture of two people in your family here.	This person is special because…	Something I like to do with this person is…
name _____		
name _____		

Amazing Animals

by _____

Draw a picture of an animal in each box. Write the name of each animal below your drawing. Then fill in the chart.

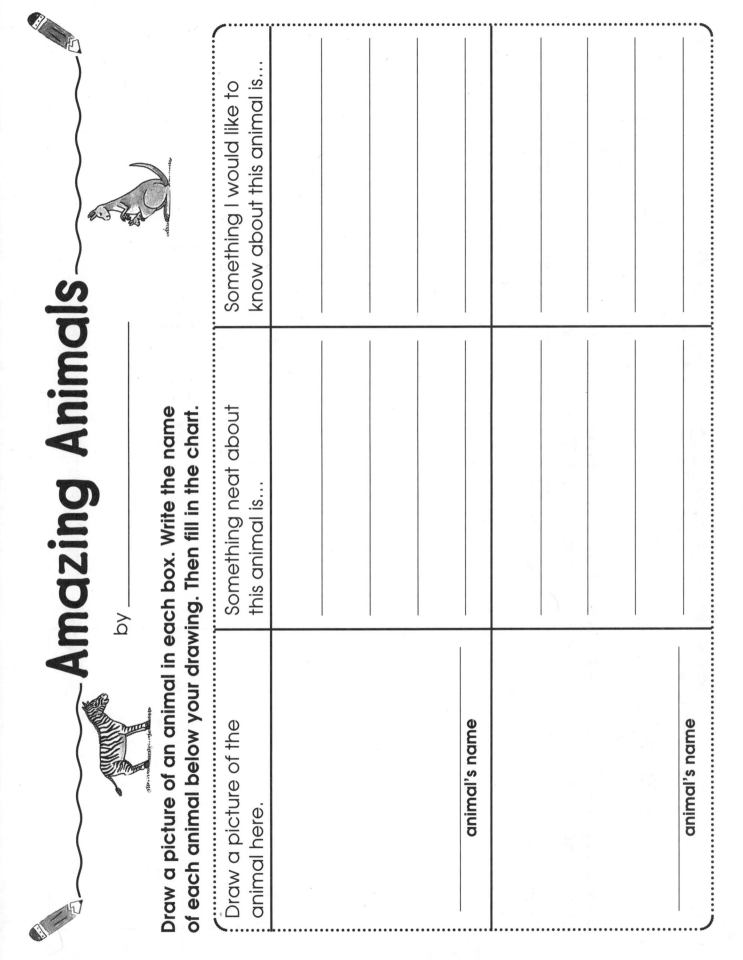

Draw a picture of the animal here.	Something neat about this animal is...	Something I would like to know about this animal is...
_____ animal's name		
_____ animal's name		

My Favorite Books

by _____

Draw a picture of one of your favorite books in each box. Write the name of each book on the line below your drawing. Then fill in the chart.

Draw a picture of the book here.	This book is about....	My favorite part of this book was....
name		
name		

# Brushing My Teeth

by _____

How do you brush your teeth? In the boxes, draw the steps that show how you brush your teeth. Then write about the steps.

1

First, I _____

_____

2

Next, I _____

_____

3

Then, I _____

_____

4

Last, I _____

_____

Getting Ready for Bed

by _____

How do you get ready for bed? In the boxes, draw the steps that show how you get ready. Then write about the steps.

1

First, I _____

_____

2

Next, I _____

_____

3

Then, I _____

_____

4

Last, I _____

_____

Getting Ready for School

by _____

How do you get ready for school? In the boxes, draw the steps that show how you get ready. Then write about the steps.

1

First, I _____

_____

2

Next, I _____

_____

3

Then, I _____

_____

4

Last, I _____

_____

My School

 by _____

Draw a picture of your school in the box below.

These are words that describe what my school looks like:

_____

_____

My favorite place in my school is_____

_____

_____

Something special about my school is _____

_____

_____

My School Interview

by _____

You are being interviewed about school. Read each question.
Then write your answers on the lines.

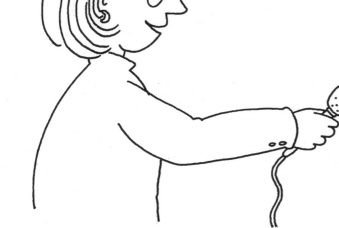

"What do you like best about school?"

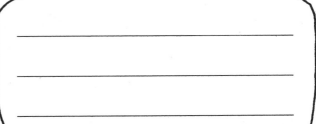

Draw yourself here. Then write your
answer in the speech balloon.

Interviewer: What are you learning in school?

Me: I am learning _____

_____

Interviewer: What is something you would like to learn about?

Me: I would like to learn about _____

_____

Happy Halloween!

by _____

In the pumpkin, draw a picture of something you do on Halloween.

In this picture, I am _____

I like to do this because _____

_____

My favorite part of Halloween is _____

_____

50 Fun-Filled Draw & Write Prompts Scholastic Professional Books

A Halloween Interview

by _____

You are being interviewed about your Halloween costume.
Read each question. Then write your answers on the lines.

"What is your costume?"

Draw yourself wearing your
Halloween costume here.
Then write your answer in the
speech balloon.

Interviewer: Why did you choose this costume?

Me: I chose this costume because _____

_____

Interviewer: What is your favorite part of your costume?

Me: My favorite part of my costume is _____

_____

My Favorite Animal

by _____

Draw a picture of your favorite animal in the box below.

My favorite animal is this color: _____

My favorite animal is bigger than a _____

but smaller than a _____

This is the noise my favorite animal makes: _____

This is where my favorite animal lives: _____

_____

My Favorite Animal Interview

by _____

You are being interviewed about your favorite animal.
Read each question. Then write your answers on the lines.

"What is your favorite animal?"

Draw yourself here. Then write your answer in the speech balloon.

Zookeeper: Why is this your favorite animal?

Me: It is my favorite animal because _____

_____

Zookeeper: What is an interesting fact about your favorite animal?

Me: An interesting fact about my favorite animal is _____

_____

My Favorite Place

by _____

Draw a picture of your favorite place in the box below.

My favorite place is _____

These are some things in my favorite place: _____

_____

_____

These are words that describe my favorite place: _____

_____

_____

My Favorite Place Interview

by _____

You are being interviewed about your favorite place.
Read each question. Then write your answers on the lines.

"What do you like to do in your favorite place?"

_____
_____
_____

Draw yourself here. Then write
your answer in the speech balloon.

Interviewer: How do you get to your favorite place?

Me: I get to my favorite place by _____

_____

Interviewer: Why is it your favorite place?

Me: It is my favorite place because _____

_____

(Draw a picture in the box.)

Happy Birthday!

2. Next, fold along this line.

1. First, fold along this line.

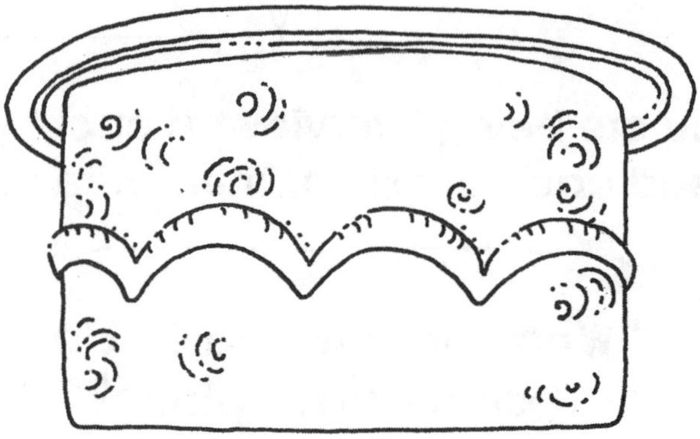

Dear _____,

This is my birthday message for you!

_____

_____

_____

_____

_____

From _____

You are _____ years old today!
(Draw the right number of candles on the cake.)

Dear ____________,

____

____

____

____

____

____

From ____________________

On Thanksgiving, I give thanks for ____________________

____

____

____

1. First, fold along this line.

Happy Thanksgiving!

(Draw a picture in the box.)

2. Next, fold along this line.

From

Dear _____ ,

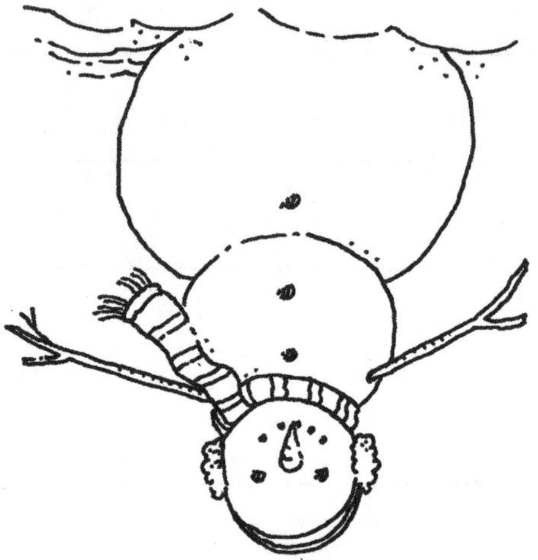

Holidays are special because

1. First, fold along this line.

2. Next, fold along this line.

Happy Holidays!

(Draw a picture in the box.)

40

_____

From

_____

_____

_____

_____

_____

Dear _____,

_____

_____

You are

Be Mine!

1. First, fold along this line.

2. Next, fold along this line.

Happy Valentine's Day!

B MINE

CBH

(Draw a picture in the box.)

From _____

_____

_____

_____

_____

_____

Dear _____,

_____

Thank you for

1. First, fold along this line.

Thank You!

2. Next, fold along this line.

(Draw a picture in the box.)

From _____

_____

_____

_____

_____

Dear _____,

Congratulations for _____

_____

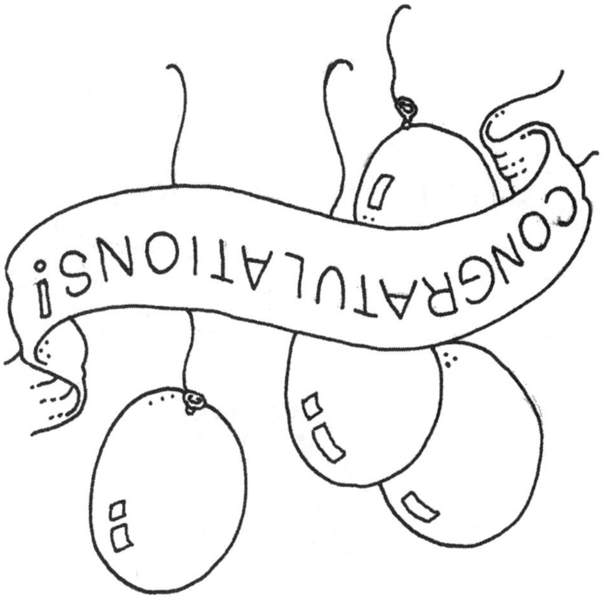

¡SNOITALUTARGNOC!

1. First, fold along this line.

Congratulations!

2. Next, fold along this line.

(Draw a picture in the box.)

Let's Share

by _____

"Give me that crayon!"

How would you answer Tim?

Think of a nice way to answer Tim, even though he did not ask nicely.

Draw a picture of yourself above.

Write what you would say in the speech balloon.

50 Fun-Filled Draw & Write Prompts Scholastic Professional Books

Making Up

by _____

"You broke my toy!"

Imagine that you have broken Samantha's toy.
What can you say to make her feel better?
Draw yourself in the box above.
Then write what you would say in the speech balloon.

Playing Together

by _____

"May I play?"

Beth is left out of the game that you are playing.

Draw yourself in the box above.

Then write what you would say to Beth in the speech balloon.

50 Fun-Filled Draw & Write Prompts Scholastic Professional Books

Be a Problem Solver!

by _____

In the box below, draw two children who are not getting along.

What is the problem the children are having?

_____

_____

What can the children do to solve their problem? What would you tell them to do?

_____

_____

A Sweet Surprise!

by _____

Use the key to color the shapes below. You will find a sweet surprise!

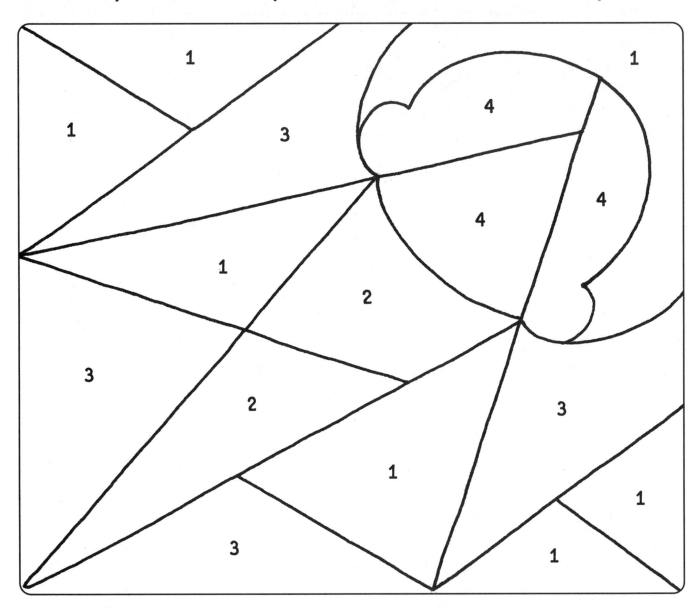

1. red

2. brown

3. green

4. yellow

This is a picture of an _____

All About Ice Cream

by _____

Draw the tallest ice cream cone you can in the box.

Write three things you know about ice cream. Use the words in the word bank if you need help.

1. _____

   _____

2. _____

   _____

3. _____

   _____

If you could invent an ice cream flavor, what would it be?

_____

_____

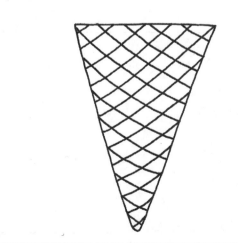

A Colorful Surprise!

by _____

Use the key to color the shapes below. You will find a colorful surprise!

1. red

2. green

3. yellow

4. blue

This is a picture of a _____

50 Fun-Filled Draw & Write Prompts Scholastic Professional Books

All About Flowers

by _____

Draw a picture of flowers growing in the flower box.

Write three things you know about flowers.
Use the words in the word bank if you need help.

1._____

_____

2._____

_____

3._____

_____

A Sports Surprise!

by _____

Use the key to color the shapes below. You will find a sports surprise!

1. yellow

2. green

3. black

4. blue

5. red

What is the girl doing in this picture? _____

_____

My Favorite Sport

by _____

What is your favorite sport?
In the box, draw a picture of you playing your favorite sport.

Write three things you know about your favorite sport.
Use the words in the word bank if you need help.

1. _____

_____

2. _____

_____

3. _____

_____

⌐ WORD BANK ⌐

goal

team

ball

field

court

run

score

net

players

A Creepy Crawly

by _____

Connect the dots from 1 to 36. Then answer the questions below.

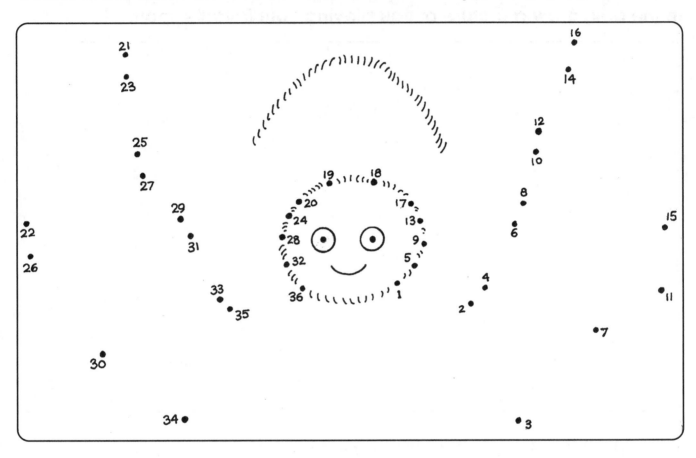

This animal is a _____.

It has _____ legs.

These are words that describe this animal:_____

_____

Would you like to have this animal as a pet?

_____

Why or why not? _____

_____

50 Fun-Filled Draw & Write Prompts Scholastic Professional Books

What a Star!

by _____

Connect the dots from 1 to 31. Then answer the questions below.

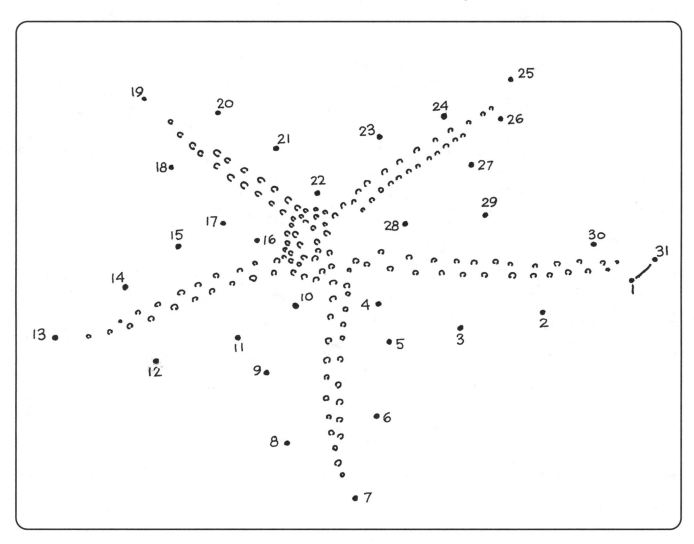

This animal is a _____.

It has _____ arms.

This animal lives _____

_____

A neat fact about this animal is _____

_____

Hanging Around

by _____

Connect the first set of dots from 1 to 30. Then connect the second set of dots from 1 to 31.

This is a picture of _____

_____

If these animals could talk, they might say, "_____

_____."

If you had these animals as pets, what would you name them?

I would name them _____ and _____

A neat fact about these animals is _____

_____

50 Fun-Filled Draw & Write Prompts Scholastic Professional Books

How to Draw a Bat

Name _____

Follow the steps to draw a bat.
Draw your bat in the box on the next page.

Step 1	Step 2

Step 3	Step 4

Step 5	Step 6

Draw & Write
About a Bat

by _____

Draw your bat in the box below.

```
........................................................
.                                                      .
.                                                      .
.                                                      .
.                                                      .
.                                                      .
.                                                      .
.                                                      .
.                                                      .
.                                                      .
.                                                      .
.                                                      .
.                                                      .
.                                                      .
.                                                      .
.                                                      .
.                                                      .
........................................................
```

Once there was a bat named _____.

He lived in a _____.

_____ liked to do many things.

He liked to _____.

But there was one thing he did not like to do.

He did not like to _____.

So instead he would _____.

50 Fun-Filled Draw & Write Prompts Scholastic Professional Books

How to Draw an Octopus

Name _____

Follow these steps to draw an octopus.
Draw your octopus in the box on the next page.

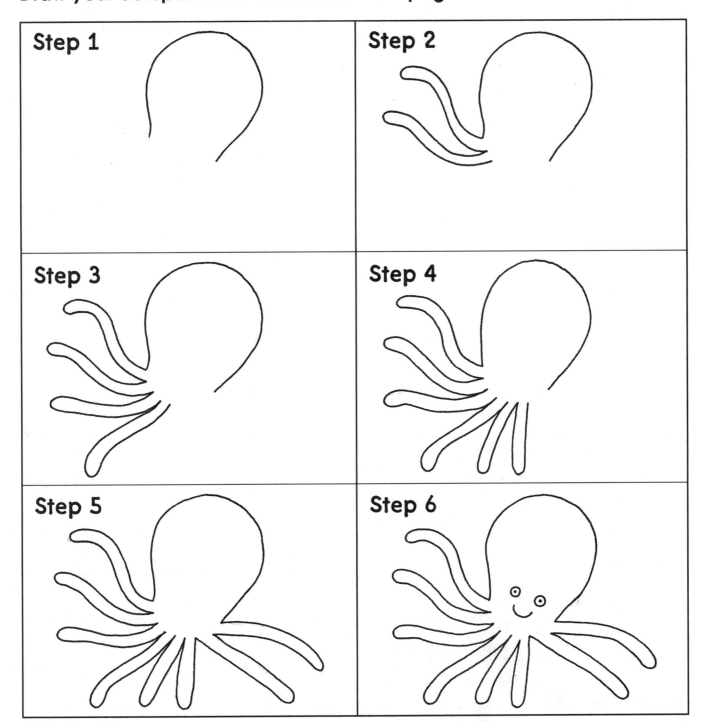

Step 1

Step 2

Step 3

Step 4

Step 5

Step 6

Draw & Write About an Octopus

by _____

Draw your octopus in the box below.

[drawing box]

Once there was an octopus named _____.

She was tired of living in the ocean.

She wanted to live in _____.

Every day she would _____.

Finally, the octopus decided to _____.

That made her feel _____.

50 Fun-Filled Draw & Write Prompts Scholastic Professional Books

How to Draw
a Giraffe

Name _____

Follow these steps to draw a giraffe.
Draw your giraffe in the box on the next page.

Step 1	**Step 2**
Step 3	**Step 4**
Step 5	**Step 6**

Draw & Write About a Giraffe

by _____

Draw your giraffe in the box below.

Once there was a giraffe named _____.

He wondered why he had such a long neck.

So he asked a very wise _____.

The wise _____ said that giraffes have long necks because

_____

_____

_____

My Imaginary Creature

by _____

This is a picture of my imaginary creature.

What is your creature's name? _____

What color is it? _____

How big is it? _____

What does it eat? _____

What special things can it do? _____

A Story About My Imaginary Creature

by _____

The title of my story is _____

In the boxes below, draw four things that happened to your creature. Then write about them on the lines.

1	2
_____ _____	_____ _____
3	**4**
_____ _____	_____ _____

50 Fun-Filled Draw & Write Prompts Scholastic Professional Books